PUFFIN BOOKS

Bill and the Ghost of Grimley Grange

Bill and the Maze at Grimley Grange

Proud of his Irish, English and New Zealand backgrounds, Anthony Stones is a leading portrait sculptor, a painter and a writer. For many years a designer with New Zealand television, he now lives in Oxford working full-time as an artist.

Bill and the Ghost
of Grimley Grange

Anthony Stones

PUFFIN BOOKS

PUFFIN BOOKS

Published by the Penguin Group
Penguin Books Ltd, 27 Wrights Lane, London W8 5TZ, England
Penguin Books USA Inc., 375 Hudson Street, New York, New York 10014, USA
Penguin Books Australia Ltd, Ringwood, Victoria, Australia
Penguin Books Canada Ltd, 10 Alcorn Avenue, Toronto, Ontario, Canada M4V 3B2
Penguin Books (NZ) Ltd, 182–190 Wairau Road, Auckland 10, New Zealand

Penguin Books Ltd, Registered Offices: Harmondsworth, Middlesex, England

Bill and the Ghost of Grimley Grange first published by Wolfhound 1988
Bill and the Maze at Grimley Grange first published by Wolfhound 1990
Published in one volume in Puffin Books 1994
3 5 7 9 10 8 6 4 2

Bill and the Ghost of Grimley Grange copyright © Anthony Stones, 1988
Bill and the Maze at Grimley Grange copyright © Anthony Stones, 1990
All rights reserved

The moral right of the author/illustrator has been asserted

Printed in England by Clays Ltd, St Ives plc

Contents

Bill and the Ghost of Grimley Grange

For Sarah Fergus and Cormac

Bill Williams felt very strange.

He wasn't used to waking in a four-poster bed, in a castle of all places.   But there he was, wearing one of Grandad's night caps and the sun just peeping in at the window.

'Rise and shine, my lucky lad,' said Grandad as he
came in with Bill's breakfast on a tray.   'Get this
inside you and then we'll have a look around the
Grange.'   He put the tray on Bill's knee.

'And if you're going to be Number Two Caretaker
you'll need a cap,' he said, and popped one on
Bill's head.

'That's his nibs, our boss, up there,' said Grandad.
'I bet he's very rich,' said Bill.

'More money than he knows what to do with,'
said Grandad. 'That's why he's off on his travels –
trying to get rid of some of it.'

Grandad went off to stoke the boiler and Bill got a good job to do . . .

'Hello!' said a voice from somewhere.

That made Bill jump!

'Not there — over here,' said the voice.

Bill looked around

. . . and got such a surprise.

'Don't be scared, Bill,' said the very strange person.   'It's only me.'
'Who's me?' said Bill.

'The Ghost of Grimley Grange of course,' said the very strange person.

'Gosh!' said Bill.   'What happened to your head?'
'Chopped off . . . what else,' said the Ghost.
'Gosh!' said Bill again.
'In my day we said *grammercy* not *gosh*,'
said the Ghost.

'When was that?' asked Bill.
'HUNDREDS of years ago,' answered the Ghost.
'GRAMMERCY,' said Bill.
'You catch on fast,' said the Ghost.

Just then they heard Grandad coming back.

'MUM'S THE WORD,' said the Ghost.   'See you later.'

'Time for lunch,' said Grandad, never suspecting a thing.

'Grandad, do you believe in ghosts?' asked Bill.
'Course not,' replied Grandad.   'No such
things.   Anyway, what makes you ask that?'
'Oh nothing,' said Bill.   'Just thinking, that's all.'
'You'd want to be careful doing that,' said
Grandad.   'Don't want to strain your brain.'

After lunch they had more work to do . . .

. . . and as they passed the picture

the Ghost gave Bill a conspiratorial wink.

They spent the afternoon picking up leaves.

Once, Bill was sure he saw the . . .

And then, as they went past a wall,

— there he was again.

'GRAMMERCY!' said Bill.

'What's that you said?' asked Grandad.

'Oh just an old-fashioned word for

gosh,' said Bill.

'My word, you're a rum lad,' said Grandad.

Then it was time to go inside.

Even Bill didn't notice who was coming along behind them.   And later, after supper,

when he was tucked up in his four-posterbed . . .

there, coming through the door that was still
SHUT, was . . .

'GRAMMERCY!', said Bill.

'Time for some adventures,' announced the Ghost.

'Where?' asked Bill.

'Well, first I've got to walk the Tower,' said the Ghost.

'What for?' queried Bill.

'I don't know, I just *have* to,' said the Ghost, '— every night.'

'*EVERY* night?' asked Bill.

'Until the end of time,' said the Ghost.

'Gosh!' said Bill, so impressed that he forgot to say his new word instead.

'Want to come?' asked the Ghost.

'Can a duck swim?' said Bill, using one of his Grandad's sayings.

'Better put on your dressing-gown and slippers,' advised the Ghost.

They tiptoed off down a corridor . . .

'I've never liked those things,' said the Ghost. 'They're what got me into this mess. Take my advice, Bill, never lose your head . . . though sometimes it has its advantages.'

They went up a spiral staircase that seemed to go
up forever, until Bill began to feel a bit dizzy.
At last they came to a big . . .

door!

The Ghost opened the door for Bill, though he himself could just have floated through it.

With a shiver, because it was even colder now, Bill found himself outside, at the top of the . . .

Tower!

'GRAMMERCY!' cried Bill.
Then, there was a terrific commotion . . . .

'I — HATE — CATS!' screamed the Ghost.

Bill made a dive
and caught the Ghost's head
just before it disappeared
over the battlements.

The poor Ghost didn't
know where he was.

'I've lost my head *again*'
was all he could say.

Then the Ghost smoothed his ruffled hair and told Bill that he had made a friend for life!

'I thought ghosts were supposed to frighten other people,' said Bill.

'If you say things like that,' said the Ghost, 'it could mean the end of a beautiful friendship.'

So Bill decided to keep his thoughts to himself. But he knew his Grandad would say it was a rum do.

'I don't feel up to walking the Tower tonight,' said the Ghost,' too much excitement. Let's go downstairs.'

'After you,' said the Ghost. 'That is if you don't mind. I'd rather not meet that cat again.'

So Bill went first. It took a long time to go down in the pitch dark, and the first thing Bill did when they got back to his room was to find the matches and light . . .

Then, you would hardly believe it . . .

the Ghost said, 'Good-night,' and was turning round to leave when he caught sight of himself in the mirror . . .

and DID IT AGAIN!

Luckily for him his head . . .

landed right on Bill's knee.

What a peculiar Ghost, thought Bill; frightened of
cats and now of HIMSELF!
'GRAMMERCY!' he said out loud.

'Bill,' said the Ghost,' I wonder if you would do me
a favour?'
'Sure,' said Bill.   'What would you like me to do?'

'Come with me to my picture,' said the Ghost.
'It's not that I'm scared or anything, it's just . . .'
'OK,' said Bill.   'Just this once though.'

'Good-night, Bill,' whispered the Ghost, 'and thanks for being such a pal.'

Then just at that moment . . .

Grandad arrived!

'Did you hear something, too, Bill?' asked
Grandad.   'I thought we had burglars.'

So Bill went off to bed and the Ghost felt safe now that he was back in his picture.

All Grandad kept saying was, 'It's a pretty rum do, Bill . . . a pretty rum do.'

Bill and the Maze at Grimley Grange

For Camilla

Bill Williams had a plan — to beat the Maze at Grimley Grange.

From his bedroom window he could see it in the moonlight.

It looked easy . . .

He would find
his way to the
middle and out again
before Grandad peeped in on the way to bed.

41

'Well — here goes,' thought Bill.

Ooops! – He had almost forgotten his ball of string.
He would need it to find his way out of the maze.

He tip-toed past Grandad's room . . .

down the stairs . . .

out of the Grange, and round the front . . .

He strode past the topiary . . .

to the entrance of the MAZE.

He tied his string to the bottom of the first shrub.

Then he set off inside, letting out the string in a trail behind him. At first . . . he did quite well.

But when he came to a dead end, he had to turn around and go back on his tracks.

Just around a corner, he heard a snuffling and a grunting . . . WAS IT A MONSTER?

But it was only a hedgehog on its nightly prowl!
When it saw Bill, it was more scared than he was
and quickly rolled itself up into

. . . a BALL.

Bill stared for ages at the
spikey bundle. But when it
didn't move, he crept carefully
around it and pressed on.

This way seemed better.

But then, if he turned around, so did the other!
And the other . . . and the other . . .

'I must make up my mind!' thought Bill.

He decided on the first way and, to his relief, came to an opening.

Lucky for Bill, he chose the one that led him almost to the middle of the maze.

Bill began to tread carefully . . .

He didn't REALLY believe in monsters . . . but just
in case there was one, it would pay to be cautious.
He put down each foot very gingerly.

He didn't notice something on the ground
and when he trod on it, there was . . .

an almighty SCREECH!!

Bill nearly jumped
out of his skin.
But it wasn't a monster.
It was the CAT!

It grabbed Bill's reel of string
and dashed away . . .

Without the string how could he find his way out?
Bill was STUCK. What a CAT-astrophe!

Meanwhile, the Ghost of Grimley Grange had stepped out of his picture frame to make his nightly walk of the tower.

Now, as you know, the Ghost of Grimley Grange hated cats. In fact, he was VERY scared of them.

When he heard the cat screech, he jumped even more than Bill had done.

He peeped over the battlements . . . and he saw the cat racing out of the maze with the string trailing from its mouth. But something else near the middle of the maze caught his eye . . .

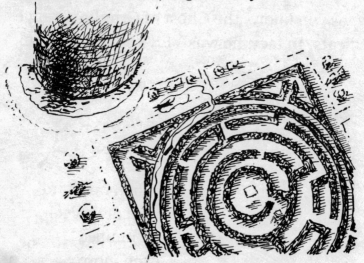

It was Bill's new paper helmet shining in the moonlight.

'But look here,' the Ghost said to himself. 'That boy was brave enough to help you once. Don't be such a COWARD. Go down this minute and help him out of the maze.'

Meanwhile Bill was trying to get out of the maze. He walked and walked and walked . . . but he kept coming to dead ends.

He tried looking under the hedges but they were too thick.

He even tried climbing to the top of the hedges but they just bent right over. Then, a cloud went over the moon . . .

A flash of lightning crossed the sky

. . . followed by a roll of thunder.

'Oh dear! Now it's going to rain as well.
I'd better hurry up,' Bill said to himself.

Suddenly, a voice said 'Hello'. 'Up here,' called
the voice.

Bill looked up and there, to his surprise, was . . .

his friend, the Ghost of Grimley Grange.

'Grammercy!' exclaimed Bill.

'That's nice,' smiled the Ghost. 'You've remembered my word.'

'How did you know I was here?' asked Bill.

'Oh, we ghosts find out what's going on,' the Ghost answered.

'But how did you know
the way?' asked Bill,
'It's so complicated.'
'Easy,' said the Ghost,

'You see, I planted the maze in the first place.
Mind you, that was *hundreds* of years ago and I'm
a bit rusty. But if I get stuck, I can do this!'

And just then . . .

another flash of lightning made them both jump.

'Grammercy! That gave me a fright,' cried the Ghost.

'And now it's going to rain,' said Bill.
'That's alright,' said the Ghost. 'Rain just goes right through ghosts. But, oh dear, you're going to be soaked.'
Bill wished he had brought his raincoat.
'Hey! I've just remembered something,' said the Ghost suddenly. 'Come over here.'

They went through the gap – and YES! . . .

They were standing right in the MIDDLE of the
maze. There was a slab of stone on the ground.
'Give me a hand to push it,' said the Ghost.

They both pushed very hard and the stone began
to slide away, revealing . . .

a hole and steps leading down under the GROUND.

'I'd forgotten all about this,' said the Ghost. 'It was my secret passage for getting out of the castle if my enemies ever won.'

'WOW!' said Bill.

'And now let's get you out of this rain,' said the Ghost. To Bill's relief, knowing what a coward the Ghost really was, the GHOST went first.

At the bottom of the steps was the entrance to a cobwebby tunnel.

The Ghost just glided through the cobwebs but Bill had to cut them with his sword.

'The Tube!' announced Bill. 'It's just like the Tube.'

It was easy for Bill to see inside the tunnel because the Ghost lit it up.

They passed other tunnels which led off the one they were following and it seemed to Bill there was something familiar about it all.

'Aren't we going in circles?' he asked the Ghost.

'I always knew you were a bright lad,' replied the Ghost. 'What do you think is happening?'

'Well,' said Bill thoughtfully . . . 'I think it's another MAZE!'

'Right first time,' said the Ghost. 'My word, you ARE a clever lad. I did it on purpose to confuse my enemies and slow them down if they chased me out of the castle.'

'But what about the one upstairs?' asked Bill.

'Same thing,' said the Ghost. 'You can't be too careful.'

They went on for a while and Bill was thinking
about what the Ghost had said.
'But' — began Bill . . .

'But what?' asked the Ghost.
'But they caught up with you eventually – your
enemies?' said Bill.

'Oh you mean this?'
asked the Ghost,
pointing to where
his head used to be.

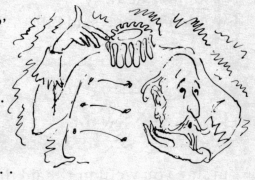

'I'd rather not talk
about *that*. It's a . . .

VERY painful subject.'

'Sorry,' said Bill. 'I didn't mean to upset you.'

'Mind you, if I'd had brave chaps like you with me it might never have happened,' said the Ghost. 'My lot all ran away.'

'I wouldn't have,' said Bill.

'I'm sure you wouldn't,' said the Ghost.

They went round one more corner and up some
steps . . . and the Ghost said: 'Well, here we are.'
But all Bill could see was a blank wall.

'Watch this,' said the Ghost. He pressed his
finger on a carved flower . . .
and the wall opened.

'FAN-TAS-TIC!' said Bill.

'Quite so,' said the Ghost.
When they stepped through,
Bill got an even bigger
surprise.

They were INSIDE Grimley Grange. And there, on the other side of the wall, was the Ghost's picture.

'SURPRISED?' smiled the Ghost.

'WOW!' said Bill. 'That's A-MAZING!'

'And now, after a crack like that,' said the Ghost, 'it's straight to bed for you. Come on!'

They had to be careful going past Grandad's room.

But there he was, still watching TV.

Bill was very glad to be tucked up in his bed again.
'Thanks Ghost,' said Bill.
'That's alright,' said the Ghost, 'One good turn
deserves another, I always say,' and off he floated

through the door, back to his picture.

The next morning at breakfast time
Grandad said, 'I could have sworn
I put my ball of string just here.
I wonder where it's got to?'

Bill swallowed hard.
'Well you see Grandad,'
he began, 'It was like this . . .

Also in Young Puffin

The
Village Dinosaur

Phyllis Arkle

"What's going on?"
"Something exciting!"
"Where?"
"Down at the old quarry."

It isn't every small boy who finds a living
dinosaur buried in a quarry, just as it
isn't every dinosaur that discovers Roman
remains and stops train smashes. Never
have so many exciting and improbable
things happened in one quiet village!

IT'S TOO FRIGHTENING FOR ME!

Shirley Hughes

"It's a spook...! There's a horrible witch in there. Don't let's *ever* go there again, Jim."

The eerie old house gives Jim and Arthur the creeps. But somehow they just can't resist poking around it, even when a mysterious white face appears at the window!

Also in Young Puffin

THE GHOST

FAMILY ROBINSON

Martin Waddell

"You know the Robinsons don't like being lonely," I said. "They'd be frightened in your house, all on their own."

The Robinsons are not ghosts who like being left alone. And they don't like not being believed in either, as Tom's parents find out when the Robinsons come to stay.

Also in Young Puffin

GRIMBLEGRAW
and the
WUTHERING WITCH

Barbara Sleigh

**"I don't like being stuffed in someone's dusty old pocket," said the Princess.
"Nor do I," said the Prince.**

Forced to cook and clean for the terrible Giant Grimblegraw with the whizzing eyes, Prince Benedict and Princess Yolanda are beginning to regret ever having longed for adventure. Their only hope of escape is to outwit the wicked Wuthering Witch who is behind it all, with her eyes that can turn them to stone.